Old CULLEN and PORTSO

by
Alan Cooper

The Seafield Arms Hotel, originally called the Cullen Hotel, was built in 1822 by Colonel F. W. Grant. Early tenants were the Watson family who occupied the farm of Denside at the same time. Douglas and George Watson were involved in the business, while another brother joined the Royal Navy and rose to become Inspector General of Hospitals and Fleets. James Caird, tenant until his retirement in 1882, was mentioned in an article as 'Old Caird with tartan trews, light vest and square hat who acted the host so well, seeing passengers off and on at the Seafield Arms' (*Banffshire Journal*, 26 January 1932). After James Caird, the tenants were Donald Falconer in 1882, Mrs Falconer in 1892 and Mrs Templeton in 1894. In 1908 the hotel was sold by Caroline, Countess of Seafield to Benjamin Miller, who at the time was the owner and occupier of the Grant Arms Hotel in Cullen.

Aboyne Castle, Portsoy.

THE PUBLISHERS REGRET THAT THEY CANNOT SUPPLY
COPIES OF ANY PICTURES FEATURED IN THIS BOOK.

ACKNOWLEDGEMENTS

The author would like to thank Findlay Pirie, former postmaster in Portsoy, for providing information about the pictures on the front and back covers and page 40.

The publishers would like to thank Allan Geddes for providing the pictures that appear on pages 5, 7, 10, 11, 13, 15, 28, 33, 44, 48 and the inside back cover.

Thanks are also due to Phillimore & Co. Ltd., Shopwyke Manor Barn, Chichester, West Sussex for permission to include extracts from *A History of Clan Grant* by Lord Strathspey, published in 1983.

FURTHER READING

The books listed below were used by the author during his research. None of them are available from Stenlake Publishing. Those interested in finding out more are advised to contact their local bookshop or reference library.

Dr Alexander Cormack, *William Cramond, 1844–1907*, 1964.
William Cramond, *The Annals of Cullen, 961–1904*, 1904.
William Fraser, *The Chiefs of Grant, Vol. 1*, 1883.
Sir John Sinclair (ed.), *The Statistical Account of Scotland, 1791–1799, Vol. 16*, 1982.
The New Statistical Account of Scotland, Vol. 13, 1845.
James Slater, *Bonnie Portsoy, A Village History*, 1995.

Lord Strathspey, *A History of Clan Grant*, 1983.
Alistair and Henrietta Tayler, *Jacobites of Aberdeenshire & Banffshire in the Forty-Five*, 1928.
Duncan Wood, *Cullen, A Pictorial History*, 1986.
Duncan Wood, *Cullen, Records of a Royal Burgh*, 1991.
Banffshire Journal, weekly from 1845.
Transactions of the Banffshire Field Club, June 1896, October 1931, March 1933.

In 1368 the thanedom of Boyne, stretching from Portsoy to Banff, was granted by David I to Sir John Edmonstone of Midlothian. (Thane was a Celtic word, equivalent to earl in English). Following the marriage of the heiress, Margaret Edmonstone, to Walter Ogilvie in about 1484, the estate passed into the hands of the Ogilvies, continuing in an unbroken line from father to son for seven generations until 1709. Walter Ogilvie was a friend and adviser to James IV, and a member of the King's Council in 1489. His grandson, Sir Walter Ogilvie, was Provost of Banff in 1549 and in the following year Portsoy became a burgh of barony, during the reign of Mary, Queen of Scots. In 1566 Sir Walter's son, Alexander, married Mary Beaton, one of the queen's 'four Marys' – her beautiful ladies-in-waiting. Soon afterwards Alexander built Boyne Castle (incorrectly captioned Aboyne Castle on this postcard) to replace the former residence on the seashore about a mile away known as Craig of Boyne Castle.

INTRODUCTION

Originally Cullen and Portsoy were both in the parish of Fordyce, which also included Deskford and Ordiquhill. Cullen became a separate parish in about 1618. Like many small towns, Cullen and Portsoy were of little consequence during the Middle Ages and only began to prosper with the completion of harbours, in 1817 and 1693 respectively. Portsoy became a burgh of barony in 1550, while Cullen's early charters (now lost) included one from the reign of William the Lion (1165–1214), and another granted by Robert the Bruce dating from between 1327 and 1329.

Cullen Bay had a strategic importance at a time when there were very few safe landing places on this stretch of coast, and the threat of invasion came mainly from the north. Vikings came ashore in the year 961 and were defeated at the Battle of the Bauds by Indulfus, King of the Scots (who was however killed on the same day in an attack on another, unbroken group). At that time there was a dense forest from the shore to the Bin Hill. The King's Cairn, one mile west of Cullen House, is said to mark the place where Indulfus died.

King Edward I of England came through the Cullen area with armies in 1296 and again in 1303, and burned the wooden fort on the Castle Hill, as well as the houses to the east of it which formed a settlement known as Invercullen. The House of Invercullen was apparently a manor house which at one time was owned by Martha, Countess of Carrick, the mother of Robert the Bruce. The latter's wife, Queen Elizabeth, died there in 1327, and her bowels were buried in the church at Cullen (her body was interred in Dunfermline Abbey). When the Scottish kings granted lands to their friends and followers, Deskford and Findlater, which then included Cullen, came into the possession of the Sinclair family, while the thanedom of Boyne, which included Portsoy, was granted to Sir John Edmonstone of Midlothian by David I in 1368. After Ogilvies (father and son) married the heiresses of both the Sinclair and Edmonstone families, they became the dominant family in the area.

In 1437 Sir Walter Ogilvie of Auchleven, the sheriff of Banff, married the heiress Margaret Sinclair, daughter of Sir John Sinclair of Deskford and Findlater, thereby coming into possession of the family's estates. His descendants were raised to the peerage as Lord Ogilvie of Deskford in 1616, Earl of Findlater in 1638, and Earl of Seafield in 1701. While Sir Walter's eldest son, James, eventually inherited Deskford and Findlater, another son, also Sir Walter, married Margaret Edmonstone, daughter of Sir James Edmonstone of Boyne and Tullialian, Perthshire. The descendants of the younger Sir Walter Ogilvie owned the Boyne estate, which included Portsoy, until 1709 when Sir Patrick Ogilvie, having got into financial difficulties, sold all his property to the 1st Earl of Seafield.

The 1st Earl of Seafield, James Ogilvie, was a second son and as was traditional went into the legal profession, becoming an advocate in 1685. He subsequently entered politics, becoming President of the Parliament in Edinburgh in 1698, and Lord High Chancellor of Scotland in 1702. James Ogilvie favoured the union with England and was one of the commissioners to negotiate the Treaty of Union in 1707. He was raised to the peerage in 1698 as Lord Ogilvie of Cullen and Viscount Seafield, and became Earl of Seafield in 1701, inheriting the title 4th Earl of Findlater in 1711 when his father died. On the union with England and Scotland's loss of independence, he famously remarked 'Now there's the end of ane auld sang' (Tayler, p11).

During the eighteenth century the 2nd Earl of Seafield introduced the cultivation of flax and the weaving of this into linen to the Cullen district. There were 65 looms in Cullen in 1793, although the industry went into rapid decline after 1800. In 1811 the 4th Earl of Seafield died childless and the Ogilvie line came to an end, at which point the old title Earl of Findlater became extinct, although the Seafield line continued as it could pass through the female line. Both the estates and the title, Earl of Seafield, were inherited by Sir Lewis Grant, a grandson of Margaret Ogilvie and her husband, Sir Lodovic Grant, Chief of the Clan Grant. As Sir Lewis was 'mentally incapacitated' (Strathspey, p42), his brother, Colonel F. W. Grant, became his guardian in 1806 and managed the estates on his behalf until 1840 when Lewis died. With the death of his brother, Colonel Francis Grant then became proprietor in his own right, and also 6th Earl of Seafield. While Lewis, the 5th Earl, had spent most of his time with his sisters at Grant Lodge, the family residence in Elgin, Colonel Grant resided at Cullen House and was responsible for many improvements during those years, including the erection of a harbour and the building of a New Town during the years 1820–30. (His father, Sir James Grant, had been the founder of Grantown-on-Spey in 1766.)

'Col. Grant found most happiness in his residence on the family estates . . . he loved to superintend improvements . . . and to promote the welfare of his tenants. He was known as the largest planter of trees in Britain . . . planting 31,686,482 over an area of 8,223 acres' (Fraser, p477). 'His taste for ornamental landscape was of a high order, and the whole of the policies were re-arranged and remodelled under his personal directions. New gardens and hot houses were built and stocked; thousands of young trees were planted; new roads were made, and ornamental ponds formed' (Fraser, pp. 478–9). 'The first house [in the new town] was erected in 1820; and under the encouragement given by his Lordship, building proceeded rapidly' (Fraser, p479). 'As the founder of the present town of Cullen, his Lordship will ever hold a certain historical importance' (*Banffshire Journal*, 2 August 1853).

The Square and Grant Street, Cullen. 'The arrival of the Royal Mail coach was a great event. It arrived [at the Seafield Arms Hotel] at Cullen at two o'clock in the afternoon from Portsoy, and there was a general turn-out to welcome it and its four spanking horses and the guard with his scarlet coat. The driver carried a blunderbuss loaded, and under his feet was a box with implements for repairing wheels, etc. The mail coach came on alternate days, but on the blank days another coach came, the driver of which had a letter-bag. Boys waited the arrival of the letters, and ran to deliver them, the driver giving them a penny each for doing so. Besides the Royal Mail, the coaches were the 'Earl of Fife' from Banff to Elgin, and the 'Defiance' ' (*Banffshire Journal*, 20 January 1903).

TOWN HALL CULLEN.

While the Old Town was being demolished during the years 1820–30, the Market Cross was, in 1821, moved to the top of Castle Hill, where it remained until 1872 when it was erected in the Square of the New Town. The new Cross was designed by Mr Millar of Cullen House and incorporated the shaft of the old Cross (1696); the memorial stone was laid in June 1872 by Provost Davidson. There were plans to have a bust of the recently deceased Provost Smith in one of the niches of the Cross; he had 'himself procured almost the whole subscription required for the building, as well as taken the greatest interest in preparation of the plan, fixing the site . . . ' (*Banffshire Journal*, 7 May 1872).

Bostock and Wombwell's Menagerie was a regular visitor to both Cullen and Portsoy, and was a travelling zoo rather than a circus. The local press mentioned visits in 1892, 1905, 1908 and 1929, but there are likely to have been many others. Often schools closed early so that the children could visit the menagerie. In 1908 Countess Caroline paid the expenses for children and teachers from Cullen, Deskford and Portknockie to make a visit. 'Such visits provide great opportunity for the children by way of an object lesson and obtaining at first hand, a greater knowledge of wild animal life' (*Banffshire Journal*, 11 June 1929). In this picture, a crowd has gathered outside the show-front, and a band can be seen playing at the left of the entrance. The menagerie closed in 1931 and the animals were sold to London Zoo.

The Menagerie in the Square. The house on the right was the parish school from 1821 until 1876. 'The ranks of canvas and caravan showmen appear to be thinning rapidly, the latest to go being the well-known Bostock's Menagerie . . . I remember quite well the last visit to Banff of the original Wombwell's. The great show of 16 huge waggons, with its magnificent stud of horses, remained over a week-end and on the Sunday a rumour got abroad that one of the lions had escaped . . . A feature of show visits in those days was the never-failing stone-fight between the youth of Banff and Macduff to finish up the day's doings at the Green Banks. Many a ding-dong battle was fought'. (*Banffshire Journal*, 13 June 1933).

In the Square, looking towards Reidhaven Street. William Cramond mentioned in his school log books, in September 1875, that 'Merry-go-rounds in the Public Square interrupt work a little'. At that time the school was situated in the Square. He also mentioned that 'A scholar John Skakel got his leg broken at them' (Cormack, p31). In May and November there were the popular Term Markets when farmers hired workers for the next six months, and the school had a holiday in the afternoon for the occasion. 'There were on the west side of the Square swingboats, roundabouts, Hairy Marys, shooting galleries; on the east side and on Seafield Street, there were stalls . . . A Hairy Mary was . . . a row of heads . . . to be knocked over at the cost of 3 balls a penny' (Cormack, p26).

This Edwardian postcard is captioned 'Lord and Lady Seafield' and shows James, 11th Earl of Seafield, his wife and their daughter Nina. There was a quarrel between John, 7th Earl of Seafield and his brothers over the money inherited from their father, which led to the earl being sued in 1878. As a result of this dispute, the earl disentailed the estates (apparently somehow with his brothers' consent!). Under the Scottish Entail Act of 1685, the estates would automatically pass at death to the nearest male relative, but after being disentailed they could be willed to anybody. This change was to have a devastating effect on the Earl's brother James and his descendants. The 7th Earl had only one child, Ian, who succeeded him as the 8th Earl in 1881. However, he died unmarried in 1884, aged 32 years. In his will, the young 8th Earl left everything, including the 300,000 acre estates, to his mother, the Dowager Countess Caroline, who became the owner for the next 27 years until her death in 1911. During these years there were three Earls of Seafield who did not own the estates, starting with her brother-in-law, James, the 9th Earl (who died in June 1888), followed by his son Francis, the 10th Earl (who died December 1888), and his grandson, James, the 11th Earl.

LORD SEAFIELD ACKNOWLEDGES WELCOME TO CULLEN.

Countess Caroline's influence extended beyond her death in 1911 as her 60-page will left the estates in the hands of the Seafield Trustees until her heir reached the age of 40 years. Under this arrangement the 11th Earl should have inherited the estates in 1916. However, he was killed in 1915 at the Battle of Ypres, having been shot in the head by a sniper while in the trenches soon after his arrival in France. He was in command of the 5th Battalion, Cameron Highlanders, at the time. As a result of his early death, the Seafield Trustees continued in full control of the estates until 1946 when the earl's only child, Nina (Countess of Seafield in her own right), reached her 40th birthday. In Countess Caroline's will 'there were a large number of financial bequests and annuities to her nieces and her other relations, friends and servants, totalling some £80,000 or so' (Strathspey, p48). This picture shows the 11th Earl being met by Provost Simpson and the town council on 31 July 1912.

Francis Grant, the man who became the 10th Earl, was never expected to succeed to the title as he was fairly distant from the line of succession, his father being the fourth son of the 6th Earl. Things changed in 1884 when his cousin, Ian Charles, the 8th Earl, died aged 32 years. Early in his life Francis had joined the Royal Navy as a midshipman, and in 1870 he settled in New Zealand, where he bought a small farm, but he experienced financial difficulties and the farm had to be sold. Another business that he entered into also collapsed, and he eventually became a labourer while his wife did domestic work. Their son, the 11th Earl, came to Britain with his wife in 1899 and became an army officer soon afterwards. Though the earl (who was also 30th Chief of the Clan Grant) was due to inherit the estates after the dowager countess's death, he had no contact with them while she was alive. The only visit by the estranged family during the countess's lifetime took place in 1902 when the earl's mother and three sisters came to Cullen and stayed at the Seafield Arms. One of the sisters kept a record of the visit in her diary. The old countess sent her factor, James Campbell, who 'really wanted to know what we wanted as we had frightened the Dowager into fits. It was agreed we would call on the Dowager at 12 o'clock, but we must not speak one word on any kind of business or ask any questions . . . We all walked up . . . The Dowager soon came in, a pretty, fair and nervous little woman . . . No one had much to say and we left after half an hour' (Strathspey, p46). These pictures show the presentation of a casket and address to the 11th Earl by Col. Johnston of Lesmurdie on behalf of the estate's tenants in the Elgin and Rothes districts. They were taken on 31 July 1912.

The Ogilvies of Findlater Castle began building Cullen House in 1600 and moved in two years later. It was plundered in 1645 by the Marquis of Montrose's army and again in 1746 by the supporters of Bonnie Prince Charlie. Feeling that they might be in danger, Lord and Lady Seafield moved to Castle Grant, the home of their son-in-law, in September 1745, and stayed there until March 1746 when they joined the Duke of Cumberland in Aberdeen. Cullen House was occupied for six weeks from February, but the main attack came on 8 April. Revd James Lawtie described how he 'heard a most terrible noise of beating and breaking things and when he went in to the court, saw the charter room open, and rebels going in and coming out, and carrying off great quantities of papers, writings and other things' (Tayler, p78). When the Jacobites had gone, he entered the house and found 'all the furniture tore down and almost all carried off, chests, trunks, cabinets, presses, broken in pieces and lying opened, all the floors full of rubbish and strewed with feathers, broken mirrors, broken glass, broken china, pieces of broken wood torn down from the panels of the room, papers, parchments torn and trampled, and mixed with dust and feathers, and jelly, and marmalade, and honey . . . ' (Tayler, p79).

Servants at Cullen House, *c*.1900. The damage to the house was estimated at £8,000, and in 1753 Lord Seafield petitioned the king for compensation in either money or forfeited estates, but did not receive anything. His petition included evidence given by his servants who were in the house at the time of its occupation. Janet Guthrie, a servant, said that 'the rebels lived riotously in Cullen House for several weeks, and that even their servants had strong ale and sugar at breakfast' (Tayler, p81). Alexander Dunbar, a porter, said that 'he saw some of the rebels break open cabinets and take out quantities of valuable china, which they threw on the floor and smashed with their guns and their feet' (ibid., p81). William Reid, a cook, described how some men held 'cocked pistols at him and others threatened to cut off his ears' (ibid., p83). Revd Lawtie 'met a mounted Jacobite, who said he understood that Lord Findlater had a good many law books and he must have some of them. He compelled Mr Lawtie to show him where they were, and having secured them from the library, he rode off in great good humour bearing the strange burden' (ibid., p79).

King Edward VII was a frequent visitor to the Seafield estates for the shooting season. His first visit was to Tulchan Lodge in 1895 when he was still the Prince of Wales. 'The story is that she [Countess Caroline] had her head gamekeeper sleep under the bedroom window in case the Prince tried to visit her, as he had a reputation for 'fondness' of the opposite sex' (Strathspey, p47). In September 1909 (when this postcard view was taken in the town) the king came from Tulchan Lodge by motor car and was welcomed by the countess at the west door of Cullen House. After lunch he was shown round the house and then visited the parish church, conducted by her factor, James Campbell.

Recalling the king's 1909 visit, the *Banffshire Journal* wrote on 10 May 1910 that 'from early hours the inhabitants had been busy in decorating the streets and houses. At a quarter to four o'clock the intimation ran through the waiting crowds that His Majesty was on his way from Cullen House. Cheer after cheer heralded to those on the Square the approach of the King, and down through the long street from the school to near the harbour the shouting and cheering was taken up and continued with enthusiasm and fervour . . . the King smiled and waved his hand.'

The Coronation of King George V took place on 22 June 1911 and was celebrated in Cullen as a holiday, with a programme of events similar to those organised for Edward VII's Coronation in 1902. These included the ringing of church bells at 10.30 a.m., a royal salute from the town's guns, a public banquet in the town hall, and a procession of public bodies and schoolchildren led by the town band to Myre Park, where a picnic, with games, was held. The press mentioned that 'There will also be a large dancing board on the ground, and a string band will be in attendance' (*Banffshire Journal*, 20 June 1911). The band and the dancers can be seen in this picture.

DANCING, CORONATION PICNIC, CULLEN.

Cullen School opened in January 1876, had accommodation for 376 pupils, and cost £2,500. It replaced the parish school in the Square and the Free Church School, as well as some small schools including an infant school at 90 Seatown. Until 1904 the headmaster was William Cramond, the author of many books on local history. Cramond had been head of the school in the Square, where he 'with three male pupil teachers taught 149 pupils in one room . . . His residence was above the classroom' (Cormack, p27). The total number of pupils attending the new school in February 1876 was 392. Though attendance became compulsory in 1873, education was not free and school fees were still charged until 1890. The school leaving age was thirteen but the law was not always enforced, and sometimes pupils left to start work at the age of twelve. Truancy was a problem and the compulsory officer was sent to find offenders, but sometimes was outsmarted, as this entry in Cramond's log book shows: 'The compulsory officer reported that James Addison . . . was dead. He was entered so in the register. Today he returned to school!' (ibid., p38).

The tollhouse seen from the Cullen side. The road on the left came from Portsoy over Crannoch Hill and was made in 1820, when the tollhouse would also have been built. 1820 was the year that the building of the New Town began, hence the bend in the road going to the left. Before 1820 the Portsoy road continued straight on (i.e. behind the toll house) to the Gallow Hill and then down to the Old Town, near Cullen House. The road on the right was the Keith turnpike of 1836. Revd George Henderson wrote in May 1842 that 'The Cullen toll bar, for the Banff and Keith turnpikes . . . yields an average revenue of £150' (*New Statistical Account*). The system under which travellers had to pay for using roads was abolished in Scotland in 1883. In 1902 the tollhouse was occupied by John Bowie and was known as the Toll Bar Croft. In 1917, when occupied by Catherine Bowie, an eleven year old boy from Cullen broke in and stole five shillings and fourpence, and as a punishment received five strokes of the birch rod.

Below: St Mary's Church, Cullen. According to one report, in early Christian times 'the church of Invercullen was dedicated to St Neachtan . . . and belonged to the Abbey of Lindores' (*Banffshire Journal*, 27 June 1933). A chapel existed in Cullen in 1236 and when Queen Elizabeth, wife of Robert the Bruce, died in the village in 1327 her bowels were buried within the church and Bruce 'bequeathed the sum of £5 Scots to be paid to the chaplain in charge, for all time, for the church's prayers for the repose of her soul. This sum, I understand, is still paid by the town towards the minister's stipend' (ibid., 8 August 1933). The oldest part of the church, St Anne's Aisle, was built during the years 1536–39. Soon afterwards, Alexander Ogilvie of Findlater and Deskford added much to St Mary's, endowing it as a collegiate church. When Cullen became a separate parish early in the seventeenth century St Mary's became the parish church. The north wing was added in 1797.

Seafield United Free Church. Following the Disruption of 1843 'a small company met for worship in a carpenter's shed at Portknockie' (*Banffshire Journal Annual*, 1973, p17). Soon afterwards a church was built in Cullen and this was opened on 2 June 1844 (Portknockie got its own Free Church in 1860). The Cullen church 'was a plain drab kind of a building, but well lit with a gallery running across the eastern end' (ibid., p15). Revd William Ross became the minister in 1894 and decided that a new church was needed, proposing in 1896 that 'the present buildings be fitted up as halls for Sabbath school, bible class and week-night services [because of] the physical discomfort of the church . . . and the impossibility of satisfactory renovation except at very great expense' (ibid., p15). By 1899, £1,600 had been collected and a bazaar raised another £555. The new church (illustrated here) was opened on 29 August 1900. Holes were left in the steeple for a bell and clock, and these were both added later, the bell in 1901 and the clock in 1910.

James Campbell, who had been factor for Caroline, Countess of Seafield until her death in 1911, retired from the town council in 1912 and enclosed as a parting gift £1,000 to provide a home for the poor of the parish. By August 1914 the building in North Deskford Street (illustrated here) had been completed, but because of the outbreak of the First World War the council offered it – with Campbell's consent – to the Red Cross Society as a VAD (Voluntary Aid Detachment) hospital for wounded soldiers. Seven soldiers arrived by train in April 1915, and many more were treated in the following months until October 1916. In 1915 the local press mentioned that 'Miss Davidson, Drumore, Lady Superintendent of the Cullen Red Cross Society, has received a handsome Red Cross flag from the Great Grimsby Coal, Salt and Tanning Company, Aberdeen, for the use of the hospital' (*Banffshire Journal*, 20 July 1915).

Cullen's bowling and tennis club was opened on 2 July 1902 and cost about £400, including the pavilion. It occupied a one-acre site leased from Caroline, Countess of Seafield at £2 10s. per year on a nineteen year lease. An earlier tennis green had existed, but had been sold in 1892 as the site for a new house (Mayfield House). The original pavilion was extended in 1913 when two new tennis courts were also added, making four in total. A new pavilion was opened in June 1924, costing between £1,000 and £1,200, and new hard-surface tennis courts, the first of their type in Scotland, were opened in May 1927. The club was very popular with visitors as well as with local people. 'One has only to attend one of those delightful impromptu concerts in the Bowling Pavilion, which follow some of the matches, to see the fine social spirit that exists between the visitors and the townspeople' (*Banffshire Journal*, 30 August 1932).

The Bowling Green, Cullen

EXPRESS ARRIVING AT CULLEN STATION.

The thirteen mile section of railway from Garmouth to Tochieneal was the last part of the Elgin to Portsoy line to be completed and opened on 1 May 1886. At the time it was described as 'about the most extraordinary and expensive in Scotland' (*Banffshire Journal*, 27 April 1886). It included a long viaduct over the Spey at Garmouth, while in Cullen there was a 70-foot high viaduct at the west end of the Seatown, and another over Seafield Street and other streets. The line was welcomed by Cullen's residents, nearly 500 of whom had signed a petition in favour of it back in 1881. When they had a chance to buy shares in the new line at a meeting in the town hall, £2,080 was paid out by townspeople. Construction work began at Cullen in March 1883 and soon afterwards 200 workmen were entertained at Cullen House, in a marquee erected for the occasion. 'Lord Seafield addressed them . . . endeavouring to persuade them to abstain from all intoxicating drinks and become members of the Blue Ribbon Army . . . About 90 afterwards signed the pledge' (*Banffshire Journal*, 1 May 1883). The Earl's mother, Countess Caroline, presented the men with copies of the New Testament.

CULLEN FROM THE WEST.

As the 8th Earl of Seafield had refused to allow the railway line to run near Cullen House (or even to cross the Seafield estate's property), expensive viaducts were needed to take it round the bay instead. While work was still in progress, the earl died suddenly, aged 32 years. 'Ian Charles died at Claridges Hotel in London after an operation to relieve a slight lameness, which entailed lifting and tying an artery. He made good progress towards recovery for a few days, but suddenly he became weak and faint, and four days later expired from nervous exhaustion' (Strathspey, pp. 43–44). A curious story exists about the 3rd Earl, who succeeded to the title in 1764. 'He used to suffer bouts of madness, and when he felt one of these attacks coming on he used to lock himself in the library and throw the keys down to his factor, who had instructions to unlock the door when he considered the attack had passed. One day the factor was rather premature in releasing his master, who is said to have fallen on him and killed him. Soon after, when the Earl had been restored to his right mind he naturally felt terribly contrite and killed himself' (ibid., p78).

An eviction took place at 97 Seatown – a pub – in June 1890, and prompted events that became known as the Seatown Riots. The tenant, a Mr Harthill, had died leaving a wife and four children. His widow then married James Mitchell, a baker, and wished to continue with the pub. However, when her new husband applied for a transfer of the licence, he was opposed by his wife's former mother-in-law, Mrs Harthill, who also applied for the licence. Both applications were turned down. Mrs Harthill then tried to have the Mitchells evicted, but when the sheriff officer, Alexander McGregor, and his assistants arrived, a crowd gathered at the house and prevented them from enforcing the eviction. Fourteen policemen were sent in the next day to help the sheriff officer, but a crowd of 200 to 300 gathered in protest and McGregor and his assistants were pelted with flour and eggs. They had difficulty in breaking open the door, and after they smashed a window Mr McGregor was hit in the face by a pail, thrown from inside. Of those involved, twelve were charged with assault and/or being 'part of a riotous mob' (*Banffshire Advertiser*, 31 July 1890). Six were sent to prison, with Mrs Mitchell receiving a sentence of 60 days and her husband 42 days.

Cullen Bay and Scaur Nose

The first Methodist services in the vicinity were held in Portknockie, at the house of Elspet McGillanders, an act that incensed Cullen's Presbyterian minister so much that he denounced the McGillanders family by name from the pulpit of his church, as well as the Methodist preacher involved. The next morning 'Ann McGillanders, the daughter, was mobbed in the streets of Cullen and had to flee for her life' (*Banffshire Journal*, 12 September 1905). In 1811 Ann married George Findlay of Cullen and Methodist services were then held in their house in Cullen until a small chapel was built in 1814. 'George Findlay was practically the maker of the little old chapel . . . He was a sort of king amongst the fishermen . . . when they built the old chapel, carrying the stones in their creels, so that the place, though one of the smallest and poorest houses of worship that Methodism possessed was to him as to many of them very beautiful and sacred' (ibid.). A new Methodist church (above, right) was opened on 7 September 1905.

CASTLE TERRACE, CULLEN.

Castle Terrace was built in the 1820s, at the same time as the New Town, and was originally known as Red Row. A. P. Mustard's warehouse (above) at 22 Castle Terrace opened in 1882 and was carried on by members of the family including Annie Mustard and her daughter, Annie Lizzie. In 1928 Mrs Mustard complained to the town council about heavy traffic passing her house. 'A motor lorry which passed recently caused a picture to fall from the wall and a clock from the mantelpiece, both being damaged. Her daughter, who was sitting at the fireside at the time was injured on the arm and foot' (*Banffshire Journal*, 9 October 1928). Mrs Mustard was still corresponding with the council over eight years later when the local press mentioned 'a letter from solicitors on behalf of Mrs A. P. Mustard, 21 Castle Terrace, complaining of vibration caused to her house by traffic' (ibid., 12 January 1937).

CULLEN BAY HOTEL, CULLEN.

'Cullen has been 'dry' since 1920 when the Scottish Temperance Act came into force. To fulfil the requirements of the law there had to be a 35 per cent poll [turn-out] and a 65 per cent majority for 'no licence' before any change could take place . . . Another poll was demanded in 1923. Feeling ran high on both sides. Some prominent workers on the 'dry' side had the windows in their houses broken when the result of the poll was announced and it was found Cullen was still 'dry'. The majority was a narrow one – only six votes' (*Banffshire Journal*, 8 December 1936). The period of prohibition continued until 1936 when another poll was held, after which the *Banffshire Journal* reported on 15 December that: 'The burgh goes 'wet' by a majority of 42 votes . . . Several causes are given for the change over, but from what one can gather, the chief reason seems to be due to the creation of a new license, since Cullen went 'dry', just outside the burgh boundary [i.e. at the Cullen Bay Hotel, above]. . . . Little or no ill-feeling has been aroused as was the case on some former occasions.'

In 1641, three men were fined by the kirk session and ordered to appear before the congregation for having played golf on a Sunday. Moving on to more modern times, golf was mentioned by the local press in 1874: 'Both cricket and golf continue to be played upon our beautiful Links. We hear of some matches about to come off soon' (*Banffshire Journal*, 14 July 1874). The golf club was probably founded at about this date. It was reported soon afterwards that 'The members of the Cullen Golf Club met on the links at 11 a.m. on New Year's Day to compete for some prizes' (ibid., 4 January 1876).

THE BEACH, CULLEN

GOLF CLUB HOUSE AND SANDS, CULLEN.
Photo: Balfour,
Copyright

In May 1879 a match was played against Banff Golf Club over 21 holes, with six players on each side. The lowest score was 97, and the highest 123 (by Revd Scott, Cullen). The original course consisted of seven holes only, but two extra holes were added in 1881. Monthly competitions for a silver medal, donated by George Seivwright, began in August 1879, sometimes with as few as six golfers taking part. The course was extended to 18 holes in 1905, and a new clubhouse (upper picture) was built in 1908 to replace the original 1896 pavilion. A much larger club house (left) was opened in 1930.

24

The railway was late in coming to Cullen (1886), but when it did finally arrive it opened up the town to tourists from the south. Four years later, the local press commented: 'The town is evidently growing in favour as a summer resort, there are at present more strangers in the town than on any previous occasion' (*Banffshire Journal*, 5 August 1890). By the 1900s, visitors were coming from as far afield as the USA, Canada and Australia, and were welcomed by townspeople who let out rooms in their houses. The beach, golf course and bowling and tennis club were all popular with visitors. Commencing in 1900, a penny bus ran between the Square and the Links. 'The Royal Burgh is getting very busy with holiday makers, nearly every house having visitors', reported the *Banffshire Journal* on 12 July 1910. As the fishing industry declined, tourism became more important to the town's economy and grew rapidly, with virtually every year during the 1920s and 30s breaking the previous record for the number of visitors.

The house known as The Cliff appears to have been built in 1901: 'At the top of the cliff, another fine-looking house has been erected by Mr McLeod, overlooking the harbour' (*Banffshire Journal*, 24 December 1901). On the right of the picture are the remains of an old windmill which was used to drive a sawmill during the nineteenth century. 'One notable landmark known to the young of the early part of the century was what we called 'the doocot'. The blue doos in our time had taken possession of what my father told me was once a windmill used to power the sawmill machinery below. He used to speak of the days when the sawmill operated there, and of how my great-grandfather, Andrew Mitchell, captain and owner of the 'Swan', used to make voyages to Norway for cargoes of timber which was fed into the mill's machinery' (*Banffshire Journal Annual*, 1981, p69). In 1932 'a limelight lecture of great interest to Cullen folk was given by Mr G. W. Findlay . . . an interesting picture was that of the old windmill on the cliff with the arms of the windmill intact' (*Banffshire Journal*, 19 January 1932).

The Cliff, Cullen

AT CULLEN HARBOUR

Cullen harbour was built in 1817 at the instigation of Colonel F. W. Grant. Cramond (p90) notes that the colonel was 'induced to lay out considerably over £4,000 in the erection of a harbour, whereof one half was defrayed by him on the part of his brother, the Earl of Seafield, and the other by the Commissioners for Highland Roads and Bridges'. The harbour was repaired and extended in 1825, and in May that year the factor at Cullen House wrote to Col. Grant saying: 'The contractors are getting on with the repairs of the Cullen harbour in a very satisfactory manner. A considerable part of the head is already rebuilt, and the entrance and interior of the harbour completely cleared, and accessible to vessels' (Fraser, p478). Further improvements were carried out in 1834.

In 1883 the 8th Earl of Seafield transferred the harbour to a Harbour Board which was to act on behalf of the public; in return the earl was paid a modest sum. The board consisted of nine members, four nominated by the earl, three by the town council, and two by those paying shore dues. Soon afterwards, a new entrance was opened and the east pier was extended by about 113 feet. During a gale in 1896 this pier collapsed, blocking the entrance, but was soon repaired. In 1907 it was reported: 'The Harbour Commissioners now find that the harbour is quite insufficient to accommodate all the boats [because they are] much larger than the former boats. There are now belonging to Cullen 60 large boats, 4 drifters and about a dozen small boats, and there is a fishing population of over 1,000. Owing to the congested state of the harbour fishermen suffer serious loss and inconvenience, as the boats employed at the line fishing are often unable to get to sea, and a considerable number of boats are unable to get accommodation in the harbour and have to go elsewhere' (*Banffshire Journal*, 28 May 1907). The harbour was taken over by the council in 1911, and an extension costing £8,000 was begun in 1913.

Reddin' the Lines, Cullen.

In the early 1800s 'the Seatown and the fishing was of little consequence . . . All the boats belonged to Lord Seafield. The fishermen got £22 to build a boat, which was expected to last seven years, and this system continued even till the time that Mr Bryson became factor (i.e. 1854). In return for the price of the boat and about one acre of land, they paid his Lordship about £5 a year, being required, however . . . between Banff and Spey, to bring wood and other commodities to his Lordship. If the distance was beyond these bounds, they received payment' (*Banffshire Journal*, 20 January 1903).

Pairtin' the Catch,
Cullen Harbour.

During the second half of the nineteenth century, Cullen and Portsoy both became important fishing ports, especially in the herring fishing. 'Those who are yet com-paratively young can recall a time when fishing arrange-ments were altogether different from those that now obtain. There was an early herring fishing at Stornoway; that was followed by the summer herring fishing on the east coast. At its close a trip was made to the Inverness or Beauly Firths for mussels, which were taken home and deposited in scalps by the seashore, and these supplied bait for the haddock fishing until Stornoway again called on the energies of the east coast men. That was the regular and well understood arrangement for the year, broken into in some cases by a few weeks of spring being spent at the great-lines, when boats after three or four days at sea, landed their catches of cod and ling, etc., making as a rule, in this case, one trip per week. That is all changed. There are fishermen now – very many of them indeed – who do not own a line. The herring is King. Its pursuit occupies the whole year round. In search of it crews go to seas that twenty years ago they seldom or never saw' (*Banffshire Journal*, 9 April 1907).

TWO OLD SALTS, CULLEN

'IS THAT OOR BOAT? CULLEN BAY'

The fishing community reached a peak of prosperity in 1918 during the First World War. 'Large and steady incomes were derived from those drifters that were in the service of the Admiralty . . . crews who remained at the fishing received prices for their catches hitherto unheard of, and it is a matter of common knowledge that never in the history of the industry have those engaged in it been so prosperous as they are today. One result is seen in the purchase by well-to-do fishermen of the finest class of houses in the town. Some of these have changed hands at very high prices' (*Banffshire Journal*, 31 December 1918). Earlier on, during the war, it was reported that 'most of the drifters belonging to Cullen have been hired by the Government at fairly liberal terms' and the 'fishing community fully engaged . . . at Admiralty work at Cromarty or Rosyth, or on patrol duty' (ibid., 28 December 1915).

During the 1920s the herring fishing industry was hit by a slump in demand, particularly in the export market to Germany and Russia, as these countries could no longer afford to pay for fish in cash. 'Quite a number of drifters . . . will have to be laid up . . . owing to there being no market for herrings' (*Banffshire Journal*, 15 February 1921). In 1929 it was reported that 'The older wooden boats are now deteriorating rapidly . . . [and] insurance companies are now making a strict survey of the vessels before covering the risk of loss' (ibid., 8 October 1929). On 25 September 1934 the paper wrote that 'those who have decided to go [to the fishing grounds] are having difficulty getting crews'.

Founded in 1882, W. & G. Gardiner was a successful boat-building yard that produced wooden 'zulu' and 'scaffie' type sailing boats for local fishermen. In 1901, seven boats were built in the yard's large black shed (illustrated here), and four the following year. However, after launching the *Fleetwing* in April 1904 business declined because of the increasing popularity of a new type of boat, the steam drifter. The first steam drifter belonging to the Cullen fleet, the *Hyssop* (BF 1277), was built in Glasgow and had arrived in June 1903. 'Through the kindness of the owners, a party of about 200 town's people had a trip to Portsoy bay, and the weather being beautiful and the sea calm, it was much enjoyed' (*Banffshire Journal*, 30 June 1903).

EBBTIDE, CULLEN BAY.

W. & G. Gardiner decided to start building steam drifters themselves in the hope that buyers would emerge, and this enterprise proved successful. In 1906 they launched the first steam drifter built in Cullen, the *Verdant*, for Messrs. George Bruce & Sons, Portknockie. (The engines were fitted in Leith.) After this initial success, the business again ran into problems, with one boat, built in 1907, still unsold two years later. In 1911 it was reported in the press that 'Messrs. W. & G. Gardiner have built one new wooden drifter for Messrs. Gardiner, Seatown, but this class of boat does not seem to be so much in favour as those of steel, the impression being that the latter are more easily steered in a crowded harbour' (*Banffshire Journal*, 26 December 1911). The outbreak of the First World War brought boat-building to a standstill, and the Depression of the 1920s almost ended it, although the industry was revived in 1932. 'The boat-building industry has been started in Cullen with the building of a motor boat . . . It is a pleasing sight to see the vessel taking shape after a long spell of idleness in the boatyard. Cullen has already five of these boats . . . their running expenses being comparatively small as compared with the drifters' (ibid., 21 June 1932). The motor was fitted by Messrs Duncan & Sons, Cullen, and the boat, named the *Nimrod*, was launched in September 1932. (The first motor boat in Cullen, the *Excellent*, arrived in June 1914 and had two 40-horsepower twin-screw motors).

CULLEN YACHT RACE

This picture shows the yacht race held in Cullen by the Swimming and Yachting Association at their third annual regatta on 16 August 1911. (The association had been founded in August 1909). In 1911, six yachts competed over a four-mile course and the winner was Mr Rome of Banff, skipper of the *Saucy Kate*, who won a silver cup, presented by Lady Seafield, and also a medal.

Charles Marione was a Frenchman who arrived at Sunnyside in November 1920 and stayed there for almost thirteen years. Sunnyside was in a remote location outside the burgh boundary; within the burgh, the town council very quickly prosecuted any similar cases. In April 1909 Alex Mennie, a pedlar from Keith, was fined ten shillings (with the option of six days in prison) for camping on the Links without permission, having been admonished on a previous occasion when he had been lodging in the Preaching Cave. In the same year, two men who had been camping near Bore Craig on the Links were admonished. Charlie Marione became popular with both locals and tourists; one wrote on a postcard in 1928: 'This old man lives in a lonely bay about a mile from here, in a little cave house in a great rock on the shore. He lives on fish and vegetables which he grows on small patches of ground, and his little house is spotlessly clean.'

SUNNYSIDE AND CHARLIE, CULLEN.

Charlie was mentioned in the *Cullen Guide Book*, 1931, and also in an article in the *Banffshire Journal* of 15 August 1933, but this increased publicity possibly brought about his downfall. Very soon afterwards he was brought before the court in Banff, charged with 'being an alien with a registered address in Pembroke . . . [and having] failed to report his arrival to the registration officer for Banffshire within 48 hours, contrary to the Aliens Order 1920' (*Banffshire Journal*, 29 August 1933). He pled guilty and was fined £1. What had led to Charlie's arrest was a complaint that 'a large number of people had been visiting the place, with constant disturbance to Mrs Murray's cattle', and also that he had been 'breaking up and cultivating pieces of ground' (ibid.). Charlie said in court that he would go to Leith, register there, and then return to France.

Findlater Castle was built by the Sinclair family at the beginning of the fifteenth century (probably by Sir John Sinclair who was killed at the Battle of Harlaw in 1411). It was the second of three castles built by the family around that time, the others being Rosslyn and Girnigoe. Rosslyn was begun by Henry St Clair, Earl of Orkney, at the end of the fourteenth century, and Girnigoe was built by the Sinclair Earls of Caithness. Findlater Castle stood two miles east of Cullen. In 1445 Sir John Sinclair's son-in-law, Sir Walter Ogilvie, obtained a licence to build towers and fortalices on to the castle, and the Ogilvies lived there until they built Cullen House in 1600. Findlater was then abandoned.

Findlater Castle.

Crossing Crannoch Moor with wood from Crannoch Hill Wood. James Boswell and Samuel Johnson came through Cullen in August 1773 during their tour of Scotland. 'We breakfasted at Cullen. They set down dried haddocks, broiled, along with our tea. I ate one; but Dr. Johnson was disgusted by the sight of them, so they were removed. Cullen has a comfortable appearance, though but a very small town, and the houses mostly poor buildings' (Boswell, *The Journal of a Tour to the Hebrides*). During the eighteenth and nineteenth centuries, the road from Portsoy came through the Crannoch Hill Wood. 'The roads about Cullen were somewhat rough, as anyone may still realise who walks along the king's highway through the Crannoch Hill Wood, and the passengers from the south sometimes found themselves, at awkward turns, deposited on the roofs of the houses of the Wynd [Old Town], or in still more undesirable situations' (*Banffshire Journal*, 20 January 1903).

A general view of Portsoy, with Church Street running from left to right. Sir Patrick Ogilvie of Boyne Castle was a judge in the Court of Session as Lord Boyne. He built Portsoy harbour (1693) and opened up the marble quarries, c.1700. However, he also borrowed heavily to finance his enterprises, especially from his relative, the 1st Earl of Seafield, and was forced to sell all his property to the earl in 1709 to cover his debts. Sir Patrick died in 1714. His eldest son, James Ogilvie, was MP for Banffshire from 1702 until the union with England in 1707 when the Scottish Parliament was abolished. He was opposed to the union and became involved in the attempts to place the Old Pretender on the British throne. In 1708 James Ogilvie arrived with a French expedition, and was put ashore in a small boat at Gamrie to obtain a pilot, but because the seas were very rough the ships, with the Old Pretender on board, sailed away and returned to Dunkirk. A warrant was issued for Ogilvie's arrest in March 1708, but he escaped to France. He played a prominent part in the 1715 rebellion, landing in disguise at Aberdeen with the Earl of Mar's commission as Commander-in-Chief, and fighting at the battle of Sheriffmuir, where he led the attack on the right of the line. As the rebellion collapsed he escaped to France again, but his wife and family, who had returned to Boyne Castle, stayed on and were evicted in 1716 in an action brought by the Earl of Seafield. 'Lady Ogilvie of Boyne was carried out of the castle, which she had resolutely refused to quit . . . in an armchair, by two men, to the green before the castle, and when there was lifted upon a horse behind a man, and taken to the Lodging [i.e. The Ritchies, illustrated on p42]', (*Banffshire Journal*, 20 September 1938).

Seafield Terrace, Portsoy. The Free Church, in the background, was opened in June 1871 by Principal Rainy and replaced the original building which dated from 1843. St John's Episcopal Church, on the right, opened for worship in 1840, while on the other side of the street the United Presbyterian Church dated from 1866 and became the town hall in 1923. At the unification of the churches in 1929, the Free Church became known as the West Church while the 'Auld Kirk' in Seafield Street became the East Church. In 1955 the latter was closed and became the church hall, while the West Church was renamed the Portsoy Parish Church of Fordyce.

Portsoy harbour was built by Sir Patrick Ogilvie of Boyne Castle and completed in 1693. Though Ogilvie tried to obtain contributions towards the cost, he received very little help and appears to have funded the project himself. 'Within his lands and barony of Boyne there is ane convenient place for a harbour called Portsoy . . . situat in that part of the countrey where there is no safe harbour for the space of four-score myles along the coast, the petitioner intends to cause erect and built ane harbour' (written in 1679 and quoted by Alastair Tayler in *Transactions of the Banffshire Field Club*, 1933, p35). The boat in this picture is the *Colonel Moir*, built in Portsoy in 1884. Cramond (p105) mentioned that in 1898 it 'left Cullen for Leith with 30 tons of small shells, got at Logie Head, and used for poultry'. The large building behind the *Colonel Moir*'s main mast was the town house of Sir Patrick Ogilvie (later known as The Ritchies). In the eighteenth century it was used by the Episcopalians after their chapel had been burned down by the Duke of Cumberland's troops in 1746, and until they built their own church in South High Street in 1797.

A close-up view of the herring curing yard that can also be made out in the left background of the picture on the front cover. The herring are lying in their long boxes (known by their Scottish name as 'farlans') awaiting gutting, cleaning and packing into barrels by the fisher girls. After this process the coopers would take over, fixing the lids to the barrels and preparing them for export to Europe, especially to the Baltic ports.

THE NEW HARBOUR, PORTSOY.

Raphael Tuck & Sons, Ltd.
London.

The eastern part of Portsoy harbour, sometimes known as the 'new harbour', was built by Colonel F. W. Grant on behalf of his brother, the 5th Earl of Seafield. Work commenced in 1825 and was completed in 1829 at a cost of £13,700. Unfortunately, a severe storm destroyed more than half of the structure in 1839, and in 1843 a writer mentioned that it had not yet been repaired. In 1882 the 8th Earl of Seafield turned the whole of the harbour into a public company (Portsoy Harbour Company) with £9,000 in shares, selling shares worth £3,000 and retaining the rest as his own. A report in 1919 mentioned the 'inadequate state of the harbour', adding that 'none of the larger drifters care to risk coming here' (*Banffshire Journal*, 30 December 1919). In spite of the depression in the fishing industry, the town council made a proposal to buy the harbour in 1924, and again in 1928 when the ratepayers voted against the idea. However, the council proceeded with the purchase in 1932.

This building and the one pictured below were both demolished during the 1930s. 'Following a complaint by one of the adjoining proprietors, the Town Council at their last meeting decided to take down the old buildings at the harbour and a start has been made . . . on the house at the bottom of North High Street. It is regrettable perhaps from a sentimental point of view that one of the old landmarks peculiar to the place is to disappear. It is one of the picturesque buildings of old time with its two arches at the entrance and must have been of considerable importance in its day' (*Banffshire Journal*, 29 January 1935).

The Ritchies', (Town House of the Ogilvies), Portsoy.

The Ritchies was originally the town house of Sir Patrick Ogilvie, and bore the date 1696 on a lintel over one of the doorways, as well as the arms of the family. On 9 October 1934 the *Banffshire Journal* reported that: 'It was agreed that the old building at the Old Harbour head, known as 'The Ritchies', should be taken down and the material sold'.

Portsoy, View showing The Mills and Bleaching Green

What is now known as Loch Soy used to be the reservoir for the nearby mills. A report, written in 1843, gives details of the operations carried on at that time. 'The manufacture of bone manure is carried on to some extent by Mr Smith in an excellently constructed site of machinery situated near the meal mill . . . The large water wheel not only gives motion to the bone machinery but also turns two circular saws and a threshing machine, all situated under the same roof. In working the bone machinery, however, it is assisted by a fly wheel, perhaps the largest of its kind in the north, which moves on the outside of the building' (*Banffshire Journal*, 20 September 1938). The mills were taken over by William Ewing in 1888, and the main business became the milling of oats into oatmeal. There were alterations in 1912 when the steam engine was replaced by a powerful gas suction engine, and the chimney stack (seen here) was taken down. Ewing died in 1951.

Portsoy is well-known for souvenirs such as ashtrays and pendants made from Portsoy marble. Today the business is small in scale, using stones and pebbles collected from the beach. When the original business was begun by Sir Patrick Ogilvie in about 1700, the stone was quarried, and the industry must have employed many people in the beginning. Revd James Lawtie gave an account of the industry in 1790: 'There is much marble (or rather jasper) at Portsoy, quarried in the ordinary manner, and manufactured into chimney-pieces, funeral monuments, tea cups, sundials, etc. Upon the first discovery, much of it was exported to France, and it is said, there are two chimney pieces of it in the palace of Versailles, and that it became fashionable in France; but the family of Boyne overstocking the market, it went out of fashion' (*Statistical Account of Scotland*).

SEAFIELD STREET, PORTSOY

Opened on 30 July 1859, the Banff, Portsoy and Strathisla Railway ran from Grange to Banff with a branch line from Tillynaught to Portsoy. By this line, Portsoy was connected to the Aberdeen to Inverness route. At the time, Portsoy was a busy seaport and a track ran from the station at Loch Soy down to the harbour, but trade declined and this part of the line was closed in 1885. (The trackway and bridges through the town can still be seen today.) The line was extended from Portsoy to Tochieneal in April 1884 and the coastal route to Garmouth and Elgin was completed in 1886. In 1929, new access to the station was opened from Durn Road, along the north side of the track.

VIEW FROM STATION, PORTSOY.

450

During the 1920s the bus became a popular form of transport and badly affected rail revenues. On 25 June 1929, the *Banffshire Journal* reported that 'There are now 90 passenger buses passing through Portsoy daily, 45 each way'. While the public welcomed the buses for their convenience and frequency, management at the railways were enraged by the rapid growth in competition: 'A letter was read from the L. N. E. Railway enclosing a booklet on 'Fair Play For the Railways' pointing out the losses which had been incurred since the introduction of the unfair bus competition. Provost Bruce (of Portknockie) said the motor was beating the steam engine and the railways need not cry out. They had had their day' (*Banffshire Journal*, 15 March 1932).

SWIMMING POOL, PORTSOY (1)

In 1930 it was reported that 'A year or two ago the provision of a bathing pool at Sandy Pots was urged, to give a safe bathing place at all times and which would be emptied and filled with fresh sea water with every tide' (*Banffshire Journal*, 8 July 1930). A pavilion was opened in March 1934 with cubicles for bathers and also tea-rooms. The swimming pool opened in 1936 and cost about £450 to construct. Another two bathing shelters were built in 1937.

The proclamation of King George V took place on 12 May 1910 in the Square, Portsoy, following a procession from the Institute Hall led by the town's brass band and followed by the police, coastguards, Royal Field Artillery, boy scouts, provost, magistrates, councillors, clergymen, freemasons and others. After a fanfare of trumpets, Provost Peter Sutherland read the proclamation. 'God save the King' was then announced, and was followed by another fanfare and a salute by the guard of honour. The band then played the national anthem and there were cheers for King George and Queen Mary, after which the procession returned to the Institute Hall.

The Lime Kilns - Boyne, Portsoy

Lime kilns, Boyne. In 1842, the minister of Fordyce parish wrote that 'There are three lime quarries; one at the mouth of the burn of Boyne; another on the Glassaugh estate near to Sandend; and a third close by that village. The last has not been much wrought for some time. There are annually produced at the first about 13,000 barrels of lime, and at the second, about 7,000' (*New Statistical Account*). Another account, written in 1843, mentioned the 'lime works of Boyne, where there is an inexhaustible vein of limestone that has been wrought for many years by Mr Wilson of Brangan, and produces lime admirably adapted both for agricultural and building purposes' (*Banffshire Journal*, 20 September 1938).